KIRI
and the
EASTER

LUKE 23:18—24:11 FOR CHILDREN

Written by Carol Greene
Illustrated by Alice Hausner

Concordia Publishing House

CONCORDIA PUBLISHING HOUSE LTD.,

117/123 GOLDEN LANE, LONDON EC1Y OTL

Printed in England.

ISBN 0-570-06064-8

The afternoon was almost gone
from old Jerusalem.
As Kiri and his father walked,
the night breeze blew on them.

From Ethiopia they'd come,
a sunny southern land.
"We'll trade our ebony and gold
with Jewish friends," they'd planned.

A mob of people jammed the streets
all colourful and loud.
"Do you know, Father," Kiri asked,
"why there is such a crowd?"

"This is the feast of Passover,
which Jews from far and near
all gather in Jerusalem
to celebrate each year."

They trudged along the noisy street
and saw a Man pass by
who looked so gentle, yet so sad
that Kiri thought he'd cry.

Just then the Stranger turned
and smiled,
and Kiri's dark eyes shone.
"Oh, Father, that's the kindest Man
that I have ever known!"

"He did seem kind," his father said,
"but, Kiri, here we are —
the home of Jacob, my old friend.
Here's Jacob at the door!"

"Come in!" cried Jacob. "Kiri too!
Meet Jesse, my young son,
who's waited all day long for you.
Together you'll have fun.

"But now come join our Passover meal, and then we'll get some rest. Tomorrow my eager Jesse can show the city to his guest."

That Friday morning dawned bright and clear.
The boys ran out the door,
through streets and markets and alleyways—
so much they must explore!

They passed a palace gleaming bright
where people milled around
and shouted, "To the cross with Him!"
An ugly, scary sound.

"Do you know, Jesse," Kiri asked, "what this is all about?"
But Jesse frowned. "No, I don't know, but we shall soon find out.

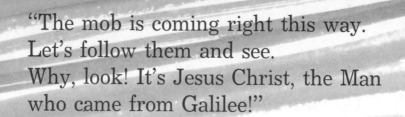

"The mob is coming right this way.
Let's follow them and see.
Why, look! It's Jesus Christ, the Man
who came from Galilee!"

Kiri and his friend were sad
to see the Lord walk by,
a heavy cross upon His back.
"He's going out to die."

A voice behind them spoke these words.
The boys turned round and saw
big Simon, Jesse's father's friend,
who shook his head in awe.

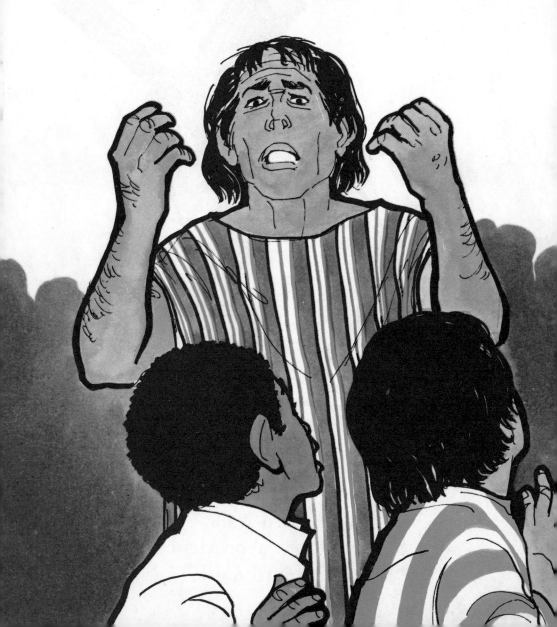

"They're killing Jesus," Simon said,
"that angry, screaming crowd."
Then Jesus turned and looked at them,
and Kiri cried out loud.

"I know Him! He once smiled at me
when He was all alone.
I thought He was the kindest Man
that I had ever known!"

A Roman guard grabbed Simon's arm.
"The Prisoner isn't strong.
Come, take the heavy cross from Him —
and you boys run along."

So Kiri and his friend went home.
The sky grew dark and drear.
"The sun is gone now," Kiri said,
"I think the end is near.

"But I don't understand at all
Why Jesus has to die.
He's such a very special Man!
Can Simon tell us why?"

At last the sky grew light again.
The two boys ran outside
to find big Simon, who might know
why Jesus had to die.

They found him standing by himself.
He gave them each a hand.
"Come sit by me and I'll explain,
for now I understand.

"Jesus was really a special Man,
the Son of God was He.
His Father sent Him to live with us
so He could set us free.

He knew He'd die upon a cross,
for that's part of God's plan.
Yet this is not the end of things—
He's going to rise again!

"The third day He'll be alive again,"
big Simon gave a nod.
"And thanks to Him all the rest of us
can live as sons of God."

The whole next day the boys could talk
of nothing but the Man
who also was the Son of God.
At last they made a plan.

And bright and early Sunday morn
they crept out to the spot
where Simon said they'd buried Him.
Would He be there or not?

They huddled close behind a rock.
Some women soon arrived.
And then two men in shining clothes
said, "He's gone. He's alive!"

"Alive!" cried Kiri, his eyes immense.
"Then Simon didn't lie!"
"I'm scared," moaned Jesse. "It's all so strange.
Do you suppose we'll die?"

"No, don't be scared. Big Simon said
it's all part of God's plan.
Since Jesus died and rose again,
death can't scare any man."

And Kiri hugged Jesse very tight.
"It's time for tears to end.
The kindest Man is the Son of God.
He'll always be our Friend."

DEAR PARENTS:

Kiri was one of those lucky people who happen to be present when something historic takes place. Your child can try to imagine how it would have been to be a witness of the crucifixion and resurrection of Jesus.

This story offers parents an opportunity to discuss the delicate subject of death. What does your child think when he hears that someone has died? Why not ask? Does the child have healthy and correct ideas about death?

Our best and dearest friends die. We shall die too. Jesus, the kindest Man, died.

Death fills us with sorrow. We feel alone and forsaken. But Jesus changed death. He broke out of death's cage when He rose from the dead. He lives again. He lives on.

We shall live again after we die — because Jesus lives again. What do you think that next life will be like? What are your child's ideas about it?

A dead friend fills us with sadness. A living friend makes us happy. Jesus is always our living Friend.

THE EDITOR